Yellowdog

Yellowdog

◆

Debra Marlin

A Bulfinch Press Book
Little, Brown and Company
Boston   New York   Toronto   London

FIRST EDITION

Part One of this book, in a slightly different version, and a portion of the photographs were previously published in
1995 under the title *Yellowdog: The Golden Retrievers of Martha's Vineyard*

LIBRARY OF CONGRESS CATALOGING-IN-PUBLICATION DATA

Marlin, Debra.
    Yellowdog / by Debra Marlin. — 1st ed.
        p.   cm.
    "A Bulfinch Press book."
    ISBN 0-8212-2343-7
    1. Photography of dogs. 2. Golden retrievers — Massachusetts —
Martha's Vineyard — Pictorial works. 3. Golden retrievers — Massachusetts —
Martha's Vineyard — Anecdotes. I. Title.
TR729. D6M37   1997
636.752'7 — dc21   96-45670

BOOK DESIGN BY JEANNE ABBOUD AND DEBRA MARLIN

Bulfinch Press is an imprint and trademark of Little, Brown and Company (Inc.)
Published simultaneously in Canada by Little, Brown and Company (Canada) Limited

PRINTED IN THE UNITED STATES OF AMERICA
PRINTED BY HULL PRINTING COMPANY
BOUND BY ACME BOOK BINDING

If you would like information on ordering limited edition prints or lithographs,
please contact Yellowdog Publishing, P.O. Box 931, Edgartown, MA 02539.

Frontispiece: Sonny and Lake

oh my yellowdog   you just don't know

how you're getting me through

the late great show.

from a song written for Sonny in 1989

S onny's in heaven," I reassured Lake as he stared into my eyes confused and upset. "I know you've heard me mention heaven to you before. It's what we lived in here together, sometimes for days at a time, without even realizing it."

Always during the darkest hours of the "night of my soul," as I referred to the torment I felt while seeking to recapture an identity I had all but lost while trying to make money instead of living my dream, I would look at my two Goldens, Sonny and Lake, and say, "Well, all is right with the world as long as I have my dogs."

It is ironic that on the day the printer called to tell me he had received the images for my first book about Sonny and Lake, Sonny's spirit chose to leave.

I felt, as one too frequently obsessed with having to have all of the answers, that it was a last fitting act of respect to forgo an autopsy. Accepting things has not been my strong suit, but I did not wish to defile his beautiful physical self. As I will for myself, I chose cremation for Sonny, and I write this as that is happening.

The second I ran over and saw him lying there as if he were asleep, I knew intuitively that his heart had burst. I knew it instantly and completely. That his sweet heart, big as it was, could not hold all of the universe's love another moment.

He died in full stride in the field I referred to as "a little piece of heaven," which was his favorite place in the world, doing his favorite thing—running as if in flight. I console myself with the knowledge that he didn't have more than one full second of suffering, and that he was with God no more after he stopped breathing than before while he was with us.

MAY 1995

7

Part One

The Story of Sonny and Lake
and how my passion for this yellowdog testament began

I t was a beautiful June day many golden summers past, and I was baby-sitting Teak, my friend Joan's dog. Teak was a majestic, full-chested Golden Retriever I had known and loved for years. My friend Maria was visiting Martha's Vineyard and helping me prepare my jewelry gallery for the summer season. We decided to play hooky and headed off to State Beach with Teak, who loved the water. The water was icy, so only Teak indulged, while Maria and I stripped to our suits and basked. Eventually Teak, having had enough, did something that for so small an act was to play a large part in my future. Cold and dripping wet and having rolled in sand, which was the obligatory act immediately following a swim, he strolled over to the wind-sheltered pit we lay in and put his huge head on my stomach. The feeling of protection and warmth that filled me was so satisfying I couldn't believe I was not minding the natural elements included in this gesture. Maria and I both ooohed simultaneously, and I looked at her and declared that I, too, must someday have a Teak-dog. That feeling was something I wanted more than just once at the beach. When Joan returned, she promised that if ever she bred Teak, I would be sure to get a puppy.

A few years went by, and my beloved Rudy, who was half German Shepherd and half St. Bernard, grew older and contracted a sudden illness. Although Rudy was master of my heart, that was not the way the general populace viewed him. He could be quite perky and social to anyone he knew, but if a stranger came near he would become vicious.

It happened that shortly before I discovered Rudy's illness, Teak sired a litter. As Rudy grew worse, I contemplated a Golden puppy. I heartily communicated to Rudy that I wished his spirit would help me pick out a puppy I could share with the world. I wanted a dog that would light up and beam warmth when he saw a person. I was sure a Golden Retriever would fill that need.

I promised Rudy that I would not let him suffer and that when he let me know I would let him go. That day came. To make my final good-byes I took him to our favorite spot at State Beach. We sat on the bluff we had visited for so many years and shared a bag of Doritos. He looked out to sea with a wistful yearning as I thanked him for all those hot afternoon swims we had enjoyed there. Then we headed back to the vet's, where I held him in my arms until he was asleep and at peace forever.

My fervent belief in the afterlife of all living things comforted me as I delivered him to the lighter, more graceful other side. I know this is something I will have to do many more times. I have made the commitment, blessed to be the receiver of so awe-inspiring a gift as the love of a dog, to be a worthy trustee of their hearts and souls until the end. The decision to entrust our hearts to a creature that most likely we will outlive is bittersweet. I'm grateful that in most cases the dogs do not have to see us go before them. I would spare them that pain.

The night Rudy died, the Golden Retrievers were born. I fell in love with an adorable, boxy-headed beauty. He molded into my arms the first time I held him and there he stayed for the rest of his life. His eyes were a fiery warm gold, matching his golden red coat, the color and brilliance of citrine. His beautiful glistening body always undulated in a dolphinlike rhythm, and when he walked toward me his toes would spread in a web, walking very gingerly so as not to disrupt anything. He grew to be a big dog, but he was grace in motion, as even in his gentle tread he tried to please.

I named him Sonny, for he was my son. His pedigree was Sundog's Golden Summer. We had many golden summers, and I was always warm and at ease with him close by.

While Sonny was a puppy, I adopted Schultz, a large, handsome German Shepherd. He raised Sonny, loving him as did I. When Sonny was two years old, Schultz died.

Sonny had so loved his big brother that after Schultz was gone, he began to manifest severe symptoms of what I eventually realized was separation anxiety. At the time, neither the vets nor I knew what was wrong. For two frightening weeks, Sonny hemorrhaged and coughed up blood, losing an enormous amount of weight.

Coincidentally, although I believe a better word would be synchronistically, a friend who knew of my passion for Goldens had dropped off a picture of her dog's father. He was majestic and glorious. In a flash of knowing, I called his champion breeder to discover he had sired a litter that was ready to be placed. I somehow understood that although the vets were testing Sonny for a few chronic diseases particular to Goldens, he was really suffering from a broken heart. The following day I got him a baby brother, Lake. He never manifested another symptom.

The dogs' bond was instantaneous. Neither dog was neutered, which meant that for several years I had two fully vital male dogs. Never once was there a snarl, snap, or so much as a hair standing up on their backs. Other male dogs, at times seeming very threatening, would surprise us on our nature walks, but there was never a dogfight. Once when we were hiking, a large skunk with its tail poised to strike walked directly in front of the three of us, looked up at me, and kept strolling. The dogs watched but did not move toward it. I'm sure the skunk recognized gentle souls. I remember that moment fondly.

As Lake healed Sonny upon their first meeting, Sonny had previously healed me. The night I took Sonny home for the first time was the beginning of a change in my life that now seems complete. The day before, I had returned from a business trip to Mexico. For about a year and a half, I had had a hard time sleeping, and the business trips seemed to complicate that problem. I was nervous, stressed, and generally unhappy, and overstimulated by what I was doing for a living. That night, I placed Sonny next to me on my bed and—for the first time in years—fell asleep instantly. During the night, I awoke to a high-pitched, frightened whimpering and found that Sonny had slipped and was wedged upside down between the bed and the wall. I retrieved him and, holding him snugly against my heart, fell asleep promising him he would never have to worry about anything in his life again. I would serve and protect and love him with all my heart. The next morning I awoke feeling like I had slept for weeks. I felt satisfied and blissful. Most important, I felt something. It had been a lifetime since I had loved anything with that intensity. I have slept and felt that way ever since. I will be eternally grateful for that miracle.

Soon after came the Christmas holidays, so we decided to take a trip off Island. Our first stop was my friend Maria's. I had to show her my Teak-dog. When I walked in with Sonny strewn over my shoulder like a sack of potatoes, everybody's eyes lit up and they screamed. He was that unutterably beautiful. On New Year's Day, Maria entered my room to find Sonny sitting in the crook of my knee. I told her that before us was the "little face of God." Surely if God could look like something of this world that we could all see and relate to, it would more than likely be a Golden Retriever. After all my years as a searcher of wisdom and truth, whose mantra was "I must cast my eyes upon beauty," I had found it in my dog's countenance and within his golden eyes. From the first time I picked him up and stared into those deeply translucent pools, I had asked, "Sonny, who are you?" He would look coyly off to one side as if to say, "Well, I can't tell you right now, but someday you'll know."

A couple of weeks before Sonny's death, after asking that question for all of his life, I held his massive, soft, square head between my hands and, peering into his soulful windows, said, "Sonny, I know who you are." He was a spirit who had come to open wide the chambers of my heart, allowing me to experience love.

Despite my awareness of his grandeur, I still often treated him like a dog. I would shoo him away and tell him he was a pain in the neck. I would scream after realizing that while I was talking to someone, he had been sliding his cold wet nose up and down my arm the entire time. This form of subliminal doggie-torture was my punishment for diverting my attention. I hope he misses my griping as much as I miss the big black nose. I have reassured myself with the thought that every "Oh, Sonny, get out of my face" was followed by "Sonny, come curl on the couch with me," or "Oh, Sonny, I love you with my whole heart and soul." The times I feel I said it best were when I would hold both dogs in a "doggie-sandwich" and whisper, "I love you everything."

The day that was to be our last together had a strange beginning. I awoke as usual with Lake taking up the bottom third of my bed. As I turned my face to the side to see the clock, there about three inches away was Sonny's nose. Some mornings, I would chide Sonny for his insistent and constant attentiveness. This was not one of those mornings. After greeting me and playing with Lake for a minute, he came around to the other side of the bed, where he stood alone. I was stroking and admiring him when he seemed to shudder. He took a big gulp and began to tremble. I was sure he must have heard thunder in the distance, as he was deathly afraid of it. However, rain had not been forecast nor was there any sign of it, so later upon rising, I decided I must have been mistaken. I took him beside me and held him as I never had, lavishing all of my love, appreciation, and comfort. These are the moments that now give me peace.

Our day progressed as usual. I did my errands particular to the beginning of the tourist season, accompanied by my two best friends. The dogs were clearly visible in my car. They featured prominently in my daily travels. I had the obligatory white Jeep with the two dogs, who were the Vineyard equivalent to the state bird. Sonny was relegated to the backseat by his little brother. He willingly took this spot for all of Lake's life, with the provision that upon our return to the house, he would be allowed to leap to the ceiling for a few minutes. While he danced through the air like a dolphin, I congratulated him on his good sportsmanship. During the day I realized that our favorite exercise routine had been delayed for several days. We would go to our field immediately following the completion of my chores. I stopped at home and received a call from my friend Debbie. We often ran our dogs together. There was an urgency in her voice as she stated that she would burst if she didn't get out for a walk, even though she didn't have her dog with her. As I drove to pick her up I thought it peculiar that she wanted to accompany us. She would never walk with us after three, and it was almost six. A creature of habit, she was breaking her routine this day.

It had been said to me by a friend's son that Lake and Sonny were distinctly different. Sonny, he noted, was an elegant gentleman, and Lake a surfer bum. Sonny was taller, with a glistening red coat and a stately square head. He had a sensitive quality in his eyes that looked as if he was considering how best to please. Lake, on the other hand, is a scamp. He is a frolicking, wide-grinned blondie who lived to tease Sonny. I don't know who would instigate it, but they wrestled with each other most of the day, every day.

Sonny's behavior at this moment was not reflecting his elegance. He was squirming and bounding around the backseat, squealing loudly. "Sonny, chill," I admonished him several times. He loved running in the field even more than going to the beach.

We arrived, and the dogs exploded like rockets from my car. We walked about half the perimeter of the field and then headed up the middle of a makeshift landing strip. Standing at the head of the strip, one could survey the entire expanse. It was at that spot that I would usually kneel and profess my gratitude for the beauty I was constantly surrounded by.

As we walked, Debbie remarked on the sky. It had a strange, enveloping cast. We approached the center of the field, where the nature paths converged with the wide-open runway. I exclaimed to Debbie that the long-missing crop circle spotted there last year had returned. Outlining a perfect circle nearly fifty feet across was a strip of grass that had a distinctly different appearance than all else around it. The grass in that foot-wide eternal band lay tilted a bit to one side, as if touched by its own gentle breeze. The band was a fluorescent Easter-basket green.

I told Debbie what I understood about those mysterious, inexplicable patterns, found primarily in England. She, too, had heard of them and appreciated the return of this exquisite piece of natural geometric art. I don't know if she believed in their sacred messages with quite my fervor, but she humored me as I ran this wide ring, laughing and inviting it to reveal its message. When I was about three-quarters of the way around the circle, I became aware of the dogs for the first time in our walk. Usually, I was hyperattentive to their exact whereabouts, being ever ready to protect them from whatever might befall them, even in this safest of all locations.

Sonny, who was all the way down at the other end of the runway, came plowing straight at me. Leaving Lake in the dust, he took me by surprise with his speed. After six years, I was still amazed at how fast and graceful he was for such a large animal. Even as he hit my legs, I was in a fog, with my mind still focused on the crop circle. My hands shot down to break the velocity of our crash, and I said as I had so many times before, in innumerable head-ons with Sonny, "Oh, Sonny, you big lummox, look out." He, seeing me frolic, had decided he wanted in on the action. I continued around the circle with Deb while Sonny ran on in the opposite direction. Suddenly, I felt a huge sucking feeling in my chest. There was a whirring, vacuum sensation in my head and chest as I looked at Deb. I remember instantly pointing to the sky and telling her that Sonny had gone. She looked quizzically at me, wondering what the joke was. I repeated to her that Sonny had gone "up there," while I pointed far up to the sky. We turned, still standing on the edge of that crop circle, and looked around. We could see him nowhere. I continued to point upward as I ran back across the field we had just come through, calling his name. I grew frantic as my conscious self caught up to what my unconscious mind already knew. In the state that had begun to be altered right before Sonny hit my legs, I ran faster and faster, calling his name. With my nearsighted, desperate eyes, I perceived a red haze lying in the distance. He was lying a bit lower than he usually did when he disappeared into the grass to chew sticks. I knew.

I came to where his body was and flashed back and forth across the threshold of actual and perceived reality. When I told Deb he was dead, she was sure I was mistaken. I gave him mouth-to-nose while motioning to her to take Lake so he wouldn't see what was happening. Debbie stood over by the crop circle, crying while she tried to calm Lake.

I had on several previous occasions looked longingly at Sonny, wishing to drink him in with my eyes so that if he were to pass, I would not feel that I hadn't looked long enough at him. I had, after all, been able to cast my eyes upon beauty, and I wanted to store it. I had tried to absorb as much of him as I could. The fact that I had let him know at every turn of my love, and his importance to me, does not diminish the amount of emotion I feel in grieving but rather completes it.

I gazed longingly at him as he lay there, to drink in more of him even at these last moments, but I could not. He had gone. He'd left without me. I knew it wasn't right to want to join him.

As I lay down each night, I had often asked God's protection for my dogs. With my prayer "Goodnight, Sonny, I love you—God bless your little soul," repeating this for Lake, myself, and God's beautiful earth, I knew I had the bases covered.

Debbie walked in tears up the field to find some help and I brought Lake over to where Sonny was. I wanted Lake to see Sonny so that he would not always be looking for him. I intuitively felt it would help. A few days later, my mother recounted an article she had just read stating that the remaining pet could accept the loss better if it could see the animal it was grieving. I'm sure now that although Lake tried himself to rouse Sonny with his paws, it was the right thing to do. Raw reality was happening, but I had a feeling that there were angels watching over us. I knew Sonny was there too. I tried to carry him back myself that mile, but there was no way I could. I knelt beside him with Lake and wept. With all my worldly power—real or imagined—I willed his blessed soul through the gilded chamber where life meets the afterlife. I'm very sure he didn't need me to do that, but it helped me. It seemed like an eternity had passed. It grew dark and I could see my white Jeep approaching from the distance.

Deb's husband, Rob, stepped from the car and with tears in his eyes solemnly embraced me. He lifted Sonny into the back, and we left our field. While driving, I remarked to Deb that it was a good thing she had been able to reach Rob. She hadn't.

Debbie had hiked the mile back to the deserted road where we had parked. She had looked for other motorists unsuccessfully and knocked on nearby doors, finding no one at home. As she stood crying on the road beside my car, Rob happened by.

I think back now to the synchronicity and protection of those moments. Sonny, generous and kind, shielded all of us, including Lake, from seeing him actually fall to the ground. A gallant knight even in death.

In the days that followed, I put myself to sleep at night trying to remember every day with Sonny in the six years we were together. I can remember most of them.

Just as Sonny gave me my voice as the original *Yellowdog* was about to go to press in May 1995, Sonny and Lake gave me my sight in October 1993, when I first began to shoot their photographs.

While in Florida during a business expansion, I became ill. I was hospitalized with an untreatable virus, and one night I "knew" that I was dying. I felt a calm I had not previously known, a release. My only concern was who would take my dogs and keep them together.

I had accidentally become more successful than I'd planned, owning several upscale jewelry galleries. It was nice living in coastal locations with a profitable business that enjoyed a cult following — but it was somebody else's life. As a friend put it, I was living a lifestyle rather than a life. I knew and accepted that I had missed the mark with my own life and career desires. I promised myself and God that if I lived, I would somehow give up my business and return to my gift as a photographer. "Please let me use my gift" became a mantra that sustained me through the worst of my illness as I systematically closed my shops. My dogs were always at my side.

While purchasing a camera at a Boston photo show, I met a blind man who furthered my desire to use the vision I feared was atrophying. With my new camera I began to focus on the dogs. They moved fast and were comely images to practice on. After a few weeks of photographing them, I began to get the knack back. It seemed appropriate to be photographing the "boys," and they soon became zealous participants. Lake was the bigger ham, always trying to be exactly a nose in front of Sonny. They would see the camera and leap into a pose.

While I closed my business down, I dove back into the study of metaphysics. I let information I had absorbed over the years flood back in. I became infused with an empathy for the human collective. I decided to call my photography project Yellowdog, hoping to add my small contribution so that others among that collective could "cast their eyes upon beauty."

I would like *Yellowdog* to stand as a symbol for all who would embrace rather than fear the inevitable changes we face as an evolving species. My hope is that this book will cross the path of fellow travelers in need of fortification as they seek the courage to give up the secure though stagnant known for the unsure but celestial light-filled new dimension.

I pray that there is a bottom to the depth of my sorrow. A week after Sonny's sudden departure, I got a baby brother for Lake. He had begun to slip into a deep depression and seems better now. The task I have taken, of writing, reading, rewriting, and editing this narrative has been almost unbearable. I have lost my son and only *thought* I knew pain before this. He was my special angel, and though I know he will live forever as that being, I miss my dog.

I love you, Sonny, with my whole heart and soul.

JUNE 1995

Part Two

———— ◆ ————

The Golden Grail

◇

A year has just passed since Sonny left us on that raw spring day at Ripley Field. I thought as I walked the familiar path there that I was right to have waited so long to return. There were no tears. It was afternoon; the tears came only late in the night. With far less frequency now did I stop and bow my head, retiring to that certain room I saved myself in. The aura in the field and my feelings that day were strange, but that was to be expected. I was relieved to find that the crop circle had completely vanished. Standing in the exact location of our event, I chose, rather than to dwell on his death, to hope that when my turn came for the trip home I would be as fortunate as my dog.

I'll follow Sonny. Somewhere in elusive Elysium he has cut a path through a golden field of light. In stillness I can catch the glint of his tail as he runs, and know that I will run with him again.

There are three dogs now. A triangulation of warm yellow fur. Tucker, now grown, saved Lake and me last summer. But Tucker and Lake were slow to bond. It was only as we left the Island to pick up yet another new puppy that they became friends. Likely the boat ride itself had something to do with this.

Halfway along the road from Edgartown to the ferry slip, my car began to buck and seize. Not a bit nonplussed after the events of the last year, I pressed forward, and convinced the boat attendants to let me on. The bronco effect was probably due to ice in the brake line. As they skeptically bullied me into my parking space on the boat I dismissed thoughts of having to turn around in Woods Hole and return to the Vineyard. Our new "boy" was being flown to Boston the following morning and I had to be there for him. Although it was early March, the temperature was forecast to drop to thirty below. The dogs and I planned to spend the night in the car at a friend's. I thought of how wonderful it would be to enfold a little swaddler in my arms again.

My projections were jarred. Suddenly the ferry and a wave equal to its size collided. The three-foot-square port window was open, and I looked up in time to see what seemed to be all of Vineyard Sound come gushing through. The deluge washed over every car as the ferry smashed into one wave and then another. As the vessel rose and fell its full height every few seconds, I was glad for the full meal I had eaten. Not wanting to miss any of this adventure, I jumped out of the car. Positioning myself behind a wide pole to watch, I vacillated between the glee of a child on the best amusement ride of her life, and the dreadful awareness that we could all drown at sea. A glance back at the Jeep confirmed what I expected I would see. Lake and Tucker were cavorting, Lake with a big grand smile, and Tucker looking a bit more apprehensive. The boat pitched and rocked uncontrollably as I gave in and delighted in my ride. I had lost myself in so many adventure fantasies over the past year, now here was the real thing. After about thirty more floodings, the attendants came to close the window. I ascended the stairs to find utter mayhem. In all directions people were spinning and weaving or lying on the deck groaning and holding their stomachs.

The sea was dark and roiling. After twelve years and hundreds of ferry trips across the sound, I had never seen the likes of this crossing. The awesome waves that smashed and broke over the boat gave me the name of my new puppy. Breaker. I'd anguished for weeks about what to call him. Eventually, knowing that when I saw him he would name himself, I let it go. He was named by the day. Breaker it was.

By the time we four arrived home on the Vineyard, Breaker was a seasoned traveler. He had flown from Houston to Boston, traveled by car the few hours it took to return to Woods Hole, and then boarded the ferry for a ride that seemed better than the previous day's only by degrees. The courage that my youngster displayed during this trip and while earning his place at home under the bossy older boys earned his complete name—Braveheart Breaker.

It is a torpidly hot June day here on the Island. Breaker turned five months yesterday. As I sit on the front lawn drawing my chronicle to a close, three beautiful, square, smiling faces peer at me from behind the screen door. Breaker, Tucker, and Lake—sometimes known as "Breaker, and Tucker, and Lake, oh my" after Dorothy's forest chant from *The Wizard of Oz*—have made my life at this moment perfect. I gaze back and wonder how I can write any more about them without succumbing to preciousness. A rationale comes easier when I think of a particular customer who wished to buy a copy of my first edition of *Yellowdog* last summer.

He filled the open double doors of my new Edgartown gallery, dressed in full sailing regalia. His booming voice matched his height as he explained that he had sailed here for the weekend. He was the CEO of a large national company and in all regards appeared bigger than life. As is my way in the shop, once we had spoken for a moment I left him alone to take in my offerings. I was framing a picture at the far end of the room when I peripherally noticed a strange motion. He was tall but stood hunched over the oak pedestal table where the book lay open. He was sobbing. As I approached and laid my hand on his shoulder, he spoke of how the story had touched him. He was not a man given to emotional displays but could feel my pain over the loss of Sonny. He told me of the immense love he felt for his own dog and how they had been together through thick and thin. His dog was very protective of him and he could not imagine his life without this regal creature. As he extracted a photo from his wallet I pictured a Great Dane or perhaps a Great Pyrenees. Much to my surprise I saw a tiny Lhasa Apso nestled atop a pillow on his couch. I laughed to myself, remembering that the small, intelligent Lhasas were used originally to protect emperors.

As people would stop to purchase a book or a print, they would share the story of their own dog with me, and depart. I would then race to the restroom to down several glasses of water, as my parched mouth hurt and I felt faint if the conversation lasted more than a few minutes. In the first few weeks of the season it was with frequency that my sadness would overwhelm me. I would fall upon the lock on the front doors and collapse behind my display case. As I released my emotions and was renewed, I would speak to the soul of my dog. In the warm southern light of my white gallery, Sonny's portraits filled me with hope. His spirit and love surrounded me. The skylight above magnified my catharsis, and in that intense June light I was rendered quiet. In the summer essences of that room I healed.

There are no pictures for the time in the winter of 1992–93, when the first inspiration for the book began. The image I must depict with words came at the beginning of my cataclysm. It is the most important picture that I did not take. I will always remember this period of my life as . . .

Sonny Underwater

I t began with a trip to the bank in the fall of 1990. There was more than one institution I was indebted to for business loans. After a midseason hurricane curtailed my retailing on the Vineyard that summer, I found myself being chastised by the financial adviser. He proceeded to advise me that the only way out of this financial dilemma was to stay permanently in Mexico while on my next silver-buying trip. I pleaded for more time to pay my debt. He became more insistent that perhaps my only option was to leave the country.

I left his office in frustration and fueled by a strong desire to show him I could pull out of the quagmire. Of course I would not run. After returning home from a jaunt with my pups, Sonny and Lake, I grabbed my most powerful tool—the telephone. Determined to repay my loans, I spent days on the phone arranging leases for two additional locations. It was done. By New Year's there would be stores in very upscale developments in Boston and on Florida's west coast.

Two winters passed and the shops were doing well. The debt that had originally propelled me into expansion grew smaller. The dogs were by my side through all of the U-Haul trips made back and forth between Florida, Boston, and Martha's Vineyard. A cavalcade of crises followed us on these journeys, yet I was not unaware of the protection I had been inexplicably blessed with.

On the first trek south, the truck engine blew up as the last bag of dog food was loaded and we were leaving Boston. Then the vehicle we'd exchanged for it died on the highway as we drove through Manhattan. Later in the trip, the car transport carrying the Jeep with the dogs inside became stuck between two gas pumps. That was just the first trip. The following year we drove down with what seemed an equal number of calamities. However, arriving at a beautiful house with a pool on the ocean made the journey seem worthwhile. And so the dogs and I settled into a routine. The cameras and other art tools I constantly swore I'd use sat covered with dust in an attractive spot in the living room.

Each day was the same. I'd let the dogs out in the morning and Sonny would throw himself upon the bubbles ascending from the pool filter. He could not explain them so he constantly sought to destroy every one. The dogs and I would sunbathe, swim, and then sun some more. I planned new stores and grew ever more chagrined that my artistic gift was not to be realized in this life. I made do with swimming with my dogs. Lake swam laps with me, proudly wrapping his paws around my neck when we were through. Sonny seemed to have become completely intimidated by the splashes his big webbed feet made as he nervously slapped the water. One day while swimming underwater I turned to find my big red dog next to me at the bottom of the pool. As if in a slow-motion ballet, Sonny gracefully swam the length, then turned to go back for more. His eyes were open and bubbles arose periodically from his nose. I was sure he was breathing.

Sonny had found his niche. Standing at the edge of the pool, I would applaud him and marvel at this near miracle. Lake would sometimes swim above him, afraid to venture lower. As he paddled he would look imploringly at me and then back at Sonny below, as if to say he wished to partake. But the deep belonged to Sonny. Sometimes as I watched I would steal a glance through the glass doors to the cameras that lay filmless on the mantel. Whenever I tried to make myself go through the door to load and shoot this awesome sight I would freeze. I was between worlds, and the world of my gift was not yet at hand. I watched and swam with Sonny, and grew greatly fatigued every time I thought of the cameras.

Looking beyond the lush blue-green foliage to the sagacious pelicans perched on the dock, I surrendered. I eventually set aside all thought of both my present retail career and my long-lost talent for photography and simply concentrated on the beauty of the moment. From the edge of the pool I would stare for hours at the palette before me. The verdant trees and cerulean sky formed a natural backdrop to the honey gold and champagne-rust of my dogs. Together we'd lie with our heads hung over the dock watching the surreal angelfish pulse their slippery water wings. The future was out of my hands. If the universe could make all of this beauty, it could certainly resolve my state of suspended animation. My worries were eclipsed by the camouflaged undulations of a skate and I wanted my future.

Driving over the Intracoastal Waterway one day, I found myself entranced by the gaiety of the dolphins playing below. I pictured a time without shops and employees and bill collectors. Then I saw myself wandering in poverty with my dogs—it was most disconcerting that this appeared to be an improvement over my present condition. I knew the end was near. I wondered if it would be the end of a chapter, or of my entire life. It wasn't my way to project a dramatic conclusion, and so I resigned myself to simply fading away. And then it happened.

A Plutonic force for inevitable change visited itself upon me in the form of an unidentified virus. When the winds of decimation were through, there would be little left of what I had known to be my life. I closed the shops. Recovery from the illness (I later found out it was one of the more deadly tick-related diseases) was slow, and bankruptcy followed. I felt as though in this loss of identity I'd divorced myself. Sonny, of course, stayed with me until the stars rang a rebirth, but little else remained, save the few thin fibers of a cellular memory. There was the gift to be used and there was Lake. If Sonny had been my angel, Lake was my cosmic steed. Many I'm sure were the lives past in which he had in one form or another pulled me to safety and been my rock. He was substantial and sturdy.

Lake. I've always loved that word. It evokes a sense of beauty in which I am at home. It is not without purpose that before retiring I cup my gentle dog's head in my hands and chant his name. As his eyes droop closed to the hushed timbre of my voice there is peace. Lake. It is the most beautiful sound I've ever heard.

Tucker is a nudge. A jackal. My moochie-poochie. Tucker tiny tot. He is my little fox-face. Truly such a boy, he is so incredibly like Sonny. I call him my needy dog. I have yet to witness him swimming underwater, but he can rub a cold nose on my arm and drive me to distraction with the best of them. Constantly fidgeting, he sleeps in the bathtub at night. If he knows I'm awake reading, he will proceed to click his toenails on the porcelain until I respond. He is smaller than most male Goldens, surely smaller than Sonny, but he packs a wallop. He's always been a great passenger in the car. However, upon my recent return to Ripley Field, here on the Vineyard, he howled and screamed as we grew near. We had driven by many open fields, but this one somehow triggered him. Although he had never been there, he knew where we were going a few miles before we arrived.

Breaker talks. Sounding like an emptying drain or a needle scratching a record, he expresses himself quite well. He is lovable but demanding. He has the unique ability to do a

360-degree turn in midair while waiting for me to prepare his dinner. He is the only one of the three who will climb up while I'm sleeping and nestle in my arms as did Sonny. What a spot he has filled for me.

The Golden Retriever is a regal beast. Secure in his own place in our hearts and in the kingdom of nature, he is gentle and wise. Recently a story was related to me of a Golden who went by the name of Jesse. The pup was gallivanting through the neighborhood with his buddy, a small terrier. They came upon the nest of a mother rabbit and her brood. Unfortunately the terrier, whose breed was originally raised to ferret out small rodents, killed all but one of the young before Jesse could intervene. Jesse returned to my friend's house delicately holding a baby in his mouth. The family raised the bunny and Jesse had a playmate.

Stories of Goldens coming to the aid of other creatures are too numerous to tell. My cupboard is filled with wonderful letters telling of their magnanimous generosity. My own recent past certainly testifies to their grace.

A baby boomer am I. A dedicated professional, I have chosen, as have so many of my peers, to raise dogs instead of children. Knowing completely and caring for these beauties has helped me to grow up.

After the first edition of *Yellowdog* appeared, a pilgrimage of movie stars, politicians, business executives, and all manner of people, found their way through my doors. Young couples and elderly folks accompanied by children and grandchildren would come in with their own Goldens in tow. They all had a story to share. It was good Island entertainment and good will. Sonny's picture on the book's cover had the same effect on others as it had had on me. That image, entitled "Waterlove," is of Sonny having just arisen from underwater. I was there with the camera waiting for him to come up for air. Growing impatient as the twilight descended I finally pulled him up. He humored me, but as soon as the shutter clicked, back down he went. The picture became a visual talisman for many of us that summer.

Alternating between the conviviality of kindred spirits and the depression/exhaustion of coping with Sonny's death, I held the vision. It was my hope that the pictures and the ability to change one's life might serve as inspiration to others.

Magic, desire, luck, love, or destiny? I grabbed and held tight. The vision rang true. People who came by shared their own losses with me. Some spoke of divorces, others of failed businesses. All used Tucker and Lake, who were always nearby, as touchstones while they related their respective changes. One evening a beautiful and serene woman came over and lightly touched my arm. As the soundtrack from *South Pacific* played in the gallery, she told me that the man singing was her husband. He had died many years before. It was clear that his love lived on. She had seen Sonny's picture in the brightly lit window and it had beckoned her in. These blessed visitors synthesized my healing. I rode bareback the powerful evidence of love yet remaining in the world, and we healed one another.

Parallel to the changes that were occurring in my life I had rekindled an interest in Arthurian lore. I began to use the quest for the Holy Grail as a metaphor for holding my own heart-centered vision. I began reading all I could find on this era and became ever more enamored of its sweet mysticism. One night I rented a movie on Camelot, the Knights of the Round Table, Arthur, Merlin, and especially Excalibur — the sword. At the end of the film the narration pledged that there would come a time when to all who lived true, with love in their hearts, the sword would reappear. The next morning I walked to the shop with Tucker and Lake coupled together like oxen at my side. As I approached the shingled building I stared in disbelief. There on the tall fence that abutted the door was a plastic toy sword. It was bright purple and had large fake jewels set into the sheath. More than bemused, I grasped the hilt and boldly unsheathed the blade. For a few days it sat in the gallery next to the stereo. There were many questions as to why the plastic sword was displayed amidst jewelry and photos that cost in the thousands. Children who came in played with it, and the dogs tried to eat it. I finally replaced it on the fence for whoever the rightful owner was, but there were no takers.

And so Excalibur found its rightful home. It is here in my house, serving as a symbol for imagination and multidimensionality. A gift had appeared and use it I must. When I clasp my hand around its fake gold mast I say yes. Yes to life, which will continue and transmutate after loss. Yes to love, which must be fostered to ascend.

It is imperative that I see my dog again in whatever form he takes.

It is paramount to the creativity once traded that I be fully here.

As a bored child in grade school, I amused myself by making what I called Island Lists. It was my version of counting sheep or meditating. I would envision myself living on a beautiful green island. I would attempt to make a list of my favorite people. These fortunate souls would accompany me to this island and we would all live happily ever after. The list, of course, never remained very small. I had done the same thing as a child when I said my prayers at night. After the first twenty names, eventually everybody was included. Everybody was blessed. And so I live here now on a beautiful green island with my dogs. It doesn't escape me that it is not only the enchanting Martha's Vineyard that I call my island home. It is my beloved Earth.

It is good for now. Here with a book, a sword, three Golden Retrievers, and a very long, unending Island List.

Thank you, Sonny, for moving the hand that I alone could never lift. Thank you for burning clear the vessel that is my heart. It is more able now to fulfill its purpose of holding the light.

JUNE 1996

Plates

Lake the Tease

Sagacious Sonny

The Dog King

Light on Lake

Poignant Lake

Apprehension

Profile of Sonny

South Beach Light

Portrait of Lake

Opposite: Dune Dog

The Dove on Lake's Chest

After the Ball

Opposite: Approaching Bliss

Lazy Afternoon

Porch Light

Sonny and Lake on Chappaquiddick

Sonny in Repose

The Chase

The Field

Opposite: Tucker's First Summer

Lake the Aloof

Lake's Little Brother

The Prayer

The Yawn

Grief

Opposite: In the Reeds

Vegetarian Retriever

Tucker's Pool

Tucker's First Swim

Breaker's Backyard

Dune Master

The Pond at the End of the Street

Tucker's Porch

Tucker's Dune

Golden Lake

Summer Idyll

Breaker, Tucker, and Lake

Breaker's Twilight Harbor

Acknowledgments

Yellowdog has been an undertaking that has flown swift and sure from the time it was first an idea. The people I would like to thank for making my dreams a reality are as follows:

My publisher at Little, Brown/Bulfinch Press, Carol Leslie, and my editor, Janet Bush. Together they have been generous to my vision and patient with my inexperience. Thanks also to Kristin Ellison, assistant editor, for making the process of this book an enjoyable experience, and to Melissa Langen and Jeanne Abboud.

Duncan Todd at Mercantile Printing. His belief in my project, tempered by a keen and conservative eye, helped shape my text. He was completely responsible for the existence of my first edition, without which this book would not have been published. I thank him as well for finding my wonderful agent.

Regina Ryan is the wonderful agent who solaced and literally supported me through the void between careers. Her stellar reputation and warm diplomacy were responsible for my creative coupling with what I consider to be the world's finest publisher of art and photography books, Little, Brown/Bulfinch.

I would like to thank Bill Nickerson, my Martha's Vineyard landlord, for the shelter he offered my dogs and me during the time before publication.

Janet Bostwick, my fine attorney at Goldstein and Manelo in Boston, guided me through the subtle nuances of a literary contract and was patient with my innumerable questions at every turn. The "tie that binds," she made the legal aspects of this project fascinating rather than intimidating.

I would like to thank David and Barbara Brown of Tempo Golden Retrievers, in Dallas, Texas, and Julie MacKinnon of Nautilus Golden Retrievers, in Plymouth, Massachusetts, from whom I received the three beauties I now call my family. Breaker, bred by the Browns, and Lake and Tucker, by Julie, are all from Champion stock, and it is remarkable that I, an unknown in the field of showing dogs, have been so fortunate as to acquire them.

In Sonny's loving memory I thank my friends Deb and Rob Young. They paid for Sonny to be cremated at a time when I could not and were there for me as no others when he died.

Thanks to Peg Thayer of Edgartown. Not only was she a great typist, she was an even better humorist when I submitted my manuscript.

Barbara Ivachek of Tisbury, Massachusetts, and Arlan Wise of Chilmark, Massachusetts, two of the world's foremost astrologers, have sustained me as I charted my life-course partially by the stars. They, along with Sandy Wand of Ashland, Oregon, were excellent spiritual counselors through my transmutation.

I am grateful to Elaine and Eli Mavros for their constant hospitality. Many is the time they offered me lodging when I journeyed from the Vineyard.

With warmth and affection I will always remember my friend Ralph Bornstein. For over a decade he has been my investor, accountant, and confidant. He died suddenly last week while helping me with an important task. His last words to me were—"Hey, Deb, give Lake a hug for me."

I would like to thank my friend Charles Chevalier for being so supportive of me in so many ways when it was time to close the shops, and helping me make the transition.